THE WRITING ON THE WALL

If Prison Walls Could Talk

BY

KY BENFORD

ISBN 979-8-9857416-2-9

Dedication

This book is dedicated to my family and friends that are racing past the walls in their lives. If I can help make a difference in anyone's life, I want it to be you. I miss you and love you. Stay blessed.

Table of Contents

Introduction
Before We Start..1

Chapter 1
A Plea Of Hope..3

Chapter 2
Musclebound 5

Chapter 3
Teardrop...8

Chapter 4
Center Stage 10

Chapter 5
Crossroad...13

Conclusion
The Last Word... 16

INTRODUCTION

~ ‿ ‿ ⁀

Before We Start

"If walls could talk…"

The statement implies that we could learn a lot from walls. On F-Block 16 Cell at the Byrd Prison Unit in Huntsville, Texas, I found this implication to be true.

As I looked around that cell from my top bunk, I observed all I could. Mainly, the walls. From those pasty walls a message of hope cried out, a teardrop fell; a musclebound man flexed; and crossroads met. But the Cross took center stage amidst the other symbols, signs, and sets[1].

Men expressed themselves.

You see, from the ancient Egyptians to the Apostle Paul; from William Shakespeare to the book you hold in your hands now, God Almighty and the human race have used the written, unwritten and illustrated word to express inspiration, feelings, warnings, direction, instruction and rebuke.

---

[1] Sets- group of linked, related or similar persons.

I have seen and read real life walls. Walls full of pain and desperation. Walls that talk. Not all walls are obvious, though. Look at a blank wall wherever you sit. It's just a wall. Or is it?

Life can be empty or puzzling as we zoom past walls to the next assignment, appointment, or bill. Caught up in the unprofitable busyness of our schedule, only tragedy, pain and breakdowns cause us to examine the walls in our lives and ask the hard question, what really matters, or where am I going in life? If we survive the shock of that tragedy, pain, and breakdown we eventually slip back into our normal lives, ignoring the hard questions.

I have had the opportunity to examine the walls in my life since living this current experience. Recognition of the walls, I surrendered to the warnings and change of direction that have evolved from this ongoing examination.

I struggle to keep my own walls standing and I cannot read the walls in your life. Whether the writing is a discreet encouragement or a bold warning, the writing is there.

Let me assure you, it doesn't take the roadblock of prison to examine walls. As you read this book, you will look into the writing I came across on the walls I saw. At the end of each chapter you will find a section called, 'The Etched Word.' Here we'll try to determine the graffiti found on your walls.

Let's read together.

CHAPTER 1

～～

A Plea of Hope

"I WILL GIVE THIS LIFE SENTENCE BACK!"

This is the statement written next to the head of the top bunk revealing someone's plea of hope.

The Bible says, 'For to him that is joined to all the living there is hope: for a living dog is better than a dead lion.' (Ecclesiastes 9:4 NKJV). The author of this scripture never saw the hopelessness of a life sentence inside prison walls. Even though he saw the hopelessness of a vain life without hope.

I don't know if the prisoner who wrote the plea ever read this Bible verse. However, hope for this or any lifer[2] is to live outside of the prison walls again.

To do that, the lifer has only a few possibilities to accomplish the feat. They include the following.

1. An appeals court overturning the case.
2. A time cut via a myriad of paperwork.
3. A Governor's pardon.
4. Escape.

---

[2] A prisoner with a life sentence.

If it reaches the extremes of desperation, this is the order of execution.

This person is putting his hope in the appeals court. Though there is little he can do to convince those people in the judicial ranks that he deserves another chance at life in society, he must continue to steer his thoughts towards hope.

As he lies on his bunk, things in his life slow down almost to a complete standstill, but his thoughts speeds on with memories, future events that he will miss, his day in court, and the big mistake. At times like this when he could use an encouraging word, he finds only a difficult and bitter cellmate. So, he checks his scrawl on the prison 'post-it' to draw another shot of reassurance.

The Etched Word

Hope is not a limited necessity to the prisoner serving a life sentence. Every one of us needs hope. The Bible says, 'Where there is no revelation, the people cast off restraint; But happy is he who keeps the law.' (Proverbs 29:18 NKJV)

Vision. Foresight. Goals. Purpose. Hope. Not all visions have substance. Without eternal purpose we become like the dog chasing his tail. The dog goes 'round and 'round chasing something he thinks he wants or needs. When (if) he catches it, he quickly realizes that what he was chasing was not what he thought it was and let go.

What are you hoping in?

CHAPTER 2

~~•~~

Musclebound

The sketch of a fourteen-inch-tall, shirtless man standing in boots and what looks like boxer's trunks, while posing in a boxer's pre-fight, weigh-in pose[3], catches my attention.

The head is a little large, disproportionate to the rest of his body with its big soft eyes and smile on his mouth. On the left pectoral muscle of the picture perfect, but under-sized body, is a tattoo of a long-horned bull.

Some people approach the intimidating place and situation of a prison just like in the sketch. The people I speak of stand physically strong in the face of adversity by doing pushups and lifting weights to try to off-set the road ahead of them. Unfortunately, the head and the egotistical pride that fills it far outweighs his physical abilities.

The body is strong, fit and ready for battle. If you choose to do hard time, there is always another opponent to entertain you until you fold.

---

[3] Double bicep flex with both arms lifted on each side.

It is said that the eyes are the gateway to the soul. Here, the big, soft eyes reveal a gentle and overwhelmed heart that is usually masked with a scowl. Knowing that the battles he should be fighting should be for better grades, a better job, and living a better life in society.

The smile on his face? It's forced. Not the bright, flashy smile but the one that says, 'I can't help but accept where I am. If I don't smile I'm going to cry.

The bull on his chest symbolizes the run of the bulls. He is going to charge at this time headfirst and aggressively with power like the bull in "El Matador." In spite of the odds, challenges, or pain, he is going to stand above this time and not be brought down by it. He will probably face quite a few bumps and bruises with this attitude, but he won't give up. Lord willing, he will survive to face the battles of a life a world away and the manhood he was designed to face…life.

The Etched Word

Prison is not all about fighting, lifting weights, and intimidation. It is said that you (each individual) makes his own time, either hard or easy, depending on his attitude.

A lot of people, but definitely not all, face prison like the muscle-bound person in the sketch. Reality is you may be facing life relying on your own strength. The struggles you are facing are overwhelming. You continue to put forth effort and spare no resource, but the struggles still prevail. As long as you continue to rely on your own strength you will not escape.

"Therefore, whoever hears these sayings of mine, and does them, I will liken him to a wise man, who built his house upon a rock and the rain

Descended, the floods came, and the winds blew, and beat on that house; and it did not fall, for it was founded upon the rock.

But everyone who hears these sayings of mine, and does not do them, will be like a foolish man who built his house on the sand: And the rain descended, the floods came, and the winds blew and beat on that house; and it fell. And great was its fall." (Matthew 7:24-27 NKJV)

Whether the house (our life) was built on The Rock (faith in Jesus) or the sand (our strength) both went through storms of tribulation. When we call upon Jesus all of our struggles disappear.

"These things I have spoken to you, that in Me you may have peace. In the world you will have tribulation; but be of good cheer, I have overcome the world." (John 16:33 NKJV)

CHAPTER 3

~~~

Teardrop

L ooming over the cell is an imposing right eye. With a teardrop starting to fall out of its outside corner, this drawing give and image and a feeling that someone is watching

If you were the eye on the wall of F21-16 cell, you would probably be watering up as well.

There has been a lot of pain and heartache that has passed its view. Any sympathetic eye would be hard-pressed not to release its tears. Broken lives, shattered dreams, severed promises, and an occasional glimpse of hope.

This isn't the only tear that has been shed here. The realization of being alone in the unforgiving 'system' with the noise, confusion, unfamiliarity and fear have all led to tears falling under the covers of the most hard-core convicts.

The eye has felt their pain; seen their struggles; and sympathized with them when no love was shared and no hope was salvaged.

Teardrops.

The eye is a drawing and an image, so is the tear, but, the pain is real.

The Etched Word

It does not take a personal prison experience to suffer or understand pain. Many people in society are living in their mental and physical prisons, bound by fear, hurt, emptiness and addiction. Hence, pain.

You know about pain. Divorce, sickness, abuse, death, and abandonment. The list goes on.

A case of free world bondage can be far worse than the loved one sentenced and sent away because their prison is evident and obvious, while the hidden prisoner's is not. Since it is hidden in its own prison, no one knows to send a card; offer help; or visit, leaving that person to face life alone.

If you are a prisoner in society, I cannot assure you that freedom comes without effort, but I can say that it comes by asking.

Then Jesus said to those Jews who believed Him, "If you abide in My word, you are My disciples indeed. And you shall know the truth, and the truth shall make you free." (John 8:31-32 NKJV)

CHAPTER 4

~ⸯⸯ ⸮~

Center Stage

The desk is made of a piece of iron fastened to the wall with very little powder blue paint left on it. The wall has some carvings and some writing on it. 'II Pac,' it says with nothing else to express that. A few more unidentifiable scribbles. 'EPT,' is in Old English font and is the initials for El Paso, Texas. A swastika sign written in red; a Diagnostics Unit address sticker; a tall Collins glass; and in the center is a cross with "He's Risen" on each side and "John 3:16" on the bottom.

II Pac or 2Pac, or Tupac Shakur, the martyred rapper and idol who some lift to god status. Putting more time and effort to know his words and history than they do to the Bible.

The Collins glass, meant for serving a mixed drink can represent the fast life. It's a way to get lost and not face reality, even though it must be faced. Even in prison the fast life is still on some people's minds.

The swastika and 'EPT' both represent things people rely on or put their trust in. Inside prison, there is safety in numbers. Men form groups based on skin color, nationality, or residence (The Hood').

The Diagnostic Unit sticker let you know that this is your reality right now. This is where you are.

Somehow, despite all the other things on the wall, and in general, the cross finds itself at the center. In the midst of reality, above all the facades; gods and scribble of this place, 'He is risen,' 'He is life,' 'He is hope.' He is what will get you through this new reality, if you call on Him. He will get you through the it.

2Pac can encourage you, make you think, and even get you 'crunk' but he cannot free himself from the grave and he cannot free me or anyone else from the bondage of sin. "How long will the mourn me?" he said on one of his songs. Some still do, but none will see him again.

The glass can be a memory of the past when you drank the emptiness away. Or, could it be the future and what you will be going back to? Alcohol, or any other vice, can numb the pain and provide a temporary escape, but it always wears off and life has to be faced.

The Etched Word

We all go through life seeking fulfillment. We find all kinds of things along the way that make us feel a part of something. This is temporary satisfaction. Whether it be a cause, club, or career, it will never fully satisfy. Only when The One who dies on the cross is given center stage in our lives will the search cease.

"And you are complete in Him, who is the head of all principality and power." (Colossians 2:10 NKJV)

CHAPTER 5

~ ~~ ~

Crossroad

A cross comforts the cell from its post on the wall opposite the bunks. Drawn in pencil, not oversized but largely present in a minuscule cell gilled with a gloomy history and somber shades of defeat. The cross brings a sense of peace. It silently, yet boldly, speaks of all things scribbled elsewhere on the walls. Time.

The cross is a landmark when it comes to time. BC (Before Christ) turned to A.D.[4] only at the birth of the bearer of the cross. Life was given at the cross. Not a life sentence in a state institution but an eternal life sentence in the Kingdom of God.

Jesus Christ served an aggravated sentence when He came to earth as God's Sacrificial Lamb, on the way to the cross to bear mankind's sin.

The Cross. Two beams. One horizontal, one vertical.

The vertical beam represents the relationship of God with man. Religion is man's attempt to reach God. Here God reaches out to man through sacrificial love.

---

[4] A.D. In the year of the Lord of the Christian era (Latin-Anno Domini).

The horizontal beam represents the distance of God's ever-ready forgiveness. "As far as the east is from the west, so far has He removed our transgressions from us." (Psalms 103:12 NKJV) An attribute that often eludes prisoners inside prison walls. Guilt and condemned is their label.

This often-misunderstood centerpiece of the cross does the same today as it did over two thousand years ago. It reminds us, even points us to The One who offers to take burden of sin from our shoulders providing peace in spite of our predicament.

The Etched Word

You have seen the cross time and again. You wear one around your neck; have them on your walls; but, have you ever sought the heart of the cross? Have you been to the ultimate crossroad where beams meet and Jesus hung?

The story has been told over may Christmas' and Easters, but has your heart really met His?

"Looking unto Jesus, the author and finisher of our faith, who for the joy that was set before Him endured the cross, despising the shame, and has sat down at the right of the throne of God." (Hebrews 12:2 NKJV)

The cross is timeless. The love of God is endless. The love of God is endless. The opportunity to take advantage of the cross and the benefits that come from Jesus is winding down. "Bless the Lord, O my soul, and forget not all His benefits." (Psalm 103:2 NKJV)

Consider this your crossroad.

CONCLUSION

~~~~~

The Last Word

I have decided that I was going to take advantage of time. In the situation I am in or any situation for that matter. I could just be killing time. I have determined that I have already done enough of that.

The Lord has blessed me with the ability to write. With that ability I wish to bless others.

We have all seen things in our lives. We all have a story to tell. The story I wanted to share with you was not necessarily of those unfortunate men in prison, but of the Prince of Peace. The One that is getting through prison. Jesus Christ.

Each year Christmas comes and goes. We go to Mass or service, spend time with families, and spend way too much money on gifts. After the season is over we each go back to our own part of the world to scratch through year.

There is more! Jesus said, "…I have come that they may have life, and that they may have it more abundantly." (John 10:10 NKJV)

I want to encourage you to take time this Christmas to not just celebrate the birth of Jesus with gifts, but to accept the ultimate gift, the gift of Salvation. Enter into a personal relationship with Jesus. "…unless one is born again, he cannot see the kingdom of God." (10:3 NKJV)

The you just read spoke of walls. Everywhere I looked on those walls shouted pain, but in those same places, the shouts were muted by the presence of Jesus.

I love you.

A BIBLICAL ACCOUNT OF THE WRITING ON THE WALL

Belshazzar the king made a great feast for a thousand of his lords, and drank wine in the presence of the thousand. While he tasted wine, Belshazzar gave the command to bring the gold and silver vessels which his father Nebuchadnezzar had taken from the temple which had been in Jerusalem, that the king and his lords, his wives, and his concubines might drink from them.

Then they brought the gold vessels that had\d been taken from the temple of the house of God which had been in Jerusalem; and the king and his lords, his wives, and his concubines drank from them. They drank wine, and praised the gods of gold and silver, bronze and iron, wood and stone.

In the same hour the fingers of man's hand appeared and wrote opposite the lampstand on the plaster the wall of the king's palace; and the king saw the part of the hand that wrote. Then the king's countenance changed, and his thoughts troubled him, so that the joints of his hips were loosened and his knees knocked against each other. The king cried aloud to bring in the astrologers, the Chaldeans, and the soothsayers. The king spoke, saying to the wise men of Babylon, "Whoever reads this writing, and tells me its interpretation, shall be clothed with purple and have a chain of gold around his neck; and he shall be the third ruler in the kingdom." Now all the king's wise men came, but they could not read the writing, or make known to the king its interpretation. Then King Belshazzar was greatly troubled, his countenance was changed, and his lords were astonished.

The queen, because of the words of the king and his lords, came to the banquet hall. The queen spoke, saying, "O king, live forever! Do not let your thoughts trouble you, not let your countenance change. There is a man in your kingdom in whom is the Spirit of the Holy God. And in the days of your father, light and understanding and wisdom, like the wisdom of the gods were found in him' and King Nebuchadnezzar your father-your father the king-made him chief of the magicians, astrologers, Chaldeans, and soothsayers. Inasmuch as an excellent spirit, knowledge, understanding, interpreting dreams, solving riddles, and explaining enigmas were found in this Daniel, whom the king named Belteshazzar now let Daniel be called, and he will give the interpretation."

THE WRITING ON THE WALL EXPLAINED

Then Daniel was brought in before the king. The king spoke, and said to Daniel, "Are you that Daniel who is one of the captives from Judah, whom my father the king brought from Judah? I have heard of you, that the Spirit of God is in you, and that light and understanding and excellent wisdom are found in you. Now the wise men, the astrologers, have been brought in before me, that they should read this writing and make known to me its interpretation, but they could not give the interpretation of the thing. And I have heard of you, that you can give interpretations and explain enigmas. Now if you can read the writing and make known to me its interpretation, you shall be clothed with purple and have a chain of gold around your neck, and shall be the third ruler in the kingdom."

Then Daniel answered, and said before the king, "Let your gifts be for yourself, and give your rewards to another; yet I will read the writing to the king, and make known to the interpretation. O king, the Most High God gave Nebuchadnezzar your father a kingdom and majesty, glory and honor. And because of the majesty that He gave him, all peoples, nations, and languages trembled and feared before him. Whomever he wished, he executed; whomever he wished, he kept alive; whomever he wished, he set up; and whomever he wished, he put down. But when his heart was lifted up, and his spirit was hardened in pride, he deposed from his kingly throne, and they took his glory from him. Then he was driven from the sons of men, his heart was made like the beasts, and his dwelling was with the wild donkeys. They fed him with grass like oxen, and his body was wet with dew of heaven, till he knew that the Most High God rules in the kingdom of men, and appoints over it whomever He chooses.

"But you his son, Belshazzar, have not humbled your heart, although you knew this. And you have lifted yourself up against the Lord of heaven. They have brought the vessels of His house before you, and you and your lords, your wives and your concubines, have drunk wine from them. And you have praised the gods of silver and gold, bronze and iron, wood and stone, which do not see or hear or know; and the God who holds your breath in His hand and owns all your ways, you have not glorified. Then the fingers of the hand were sent from Him, and this writing was written.

"And this is the inscription that was written:

MENE, MENE, TEKEL, UPHARSIN.

This is the interpretation of each word.

MENE: God has numbered your kingdom, and finished.

TEKEL: You have been weighed in the balances, and found wanting. PERES: Your kingdom has been divided, and given to the Medes and Persians.

Then Belshazzar gave the command, and they clothed Daniel with purple and put a chain of gold around his neck, and made a proclamation concerning him that he should be the third ruler in the kingdom.

That very night Belshazzar, king of the Chaldeans was slain. And Darius the Mede received, being about sixty-two years old.

Daniel 5 (NKJV)